"A good book is the best of friends, the same today and forever." —Tupper

Given for the glory of God
to the media library
in honor of

Mrs. Gail Pine

with love and deep appreciation by

Mission Friends

March 24, 1985

date

Oz and Mary Quick:
Taiwan Teammates

WILLIAM N. McELRATH

Illustrated by Mike Sloan

BROADMAN PRESS
Nashville, Tennessee

Library of Congress Cataloging in Publication Data

McElrath, William N.
  Oz and Mary Quick.

  Summary: A biography of Dr. O. J. and Mary Quick,
missionaries to Taiwan, with emphasis on how they became
missionaries, the work they do, and the people with whom
they work.
  1. Quick, Oz—Juvenile literature. 2. Quick, Mary—
Juvenile literature. 3. Missionaries—Taiwan—Biography—
Juvenile literature. 4. Missionaries—United States—
Biography—Juvenile literature. [1. Quick, Oz.
2. Quick, Mary. 3. Missionaries] I. Sloan, Michael,
1946-   , ill. II. Title.
BV3431.M34 1984   266'.61'0922 [B] [920]   84-2962
ISBN 0-8054-4287-1

Contents

"I Want to Be a Missionary"

Oz Quick tumbled out the front door at a run. He raced his brothers, J. C. and Dick, across the front porch, into the yard, across the street, and onto the school grounds.

It was the fall of 1924, and nine-year-old Oz felt like a big boy now. His curly brown hair tossed in the wind as he easily beat little Dick to the school door. But J. C. was already in high school, and his long legs got him there first.

"You fellows are still too little!" J. C. teased.

Oz was still pouting when classes started. Maybe that was why he got in a scuffle with another fourth grader. The teacher sent both boys to the principal's office.

"Wonder what he'll do to us," Oz whispered as they tiptoed down the hall.

The other boy shook his head. "They say he uses a rubber hose."

The principal let both boys off with a warning. But news spreads fast in a big family, and Oz had two brothers and three sisters then. Dad heard all about what had happened when he came in from the grain elevator to eat supper.

Oz wasn't sure where he hurt most when he went to bed that night: in his body or in his mind. He knew he had done wrong that day in school, and other days in other places. He never felt good when he disobeyed his mom or when he told a little less than the truth. He knew that doing wrong brings punishment, now or later.

On Sunday morning Mom helped the young Quicks get ready for church. Oz could hardly remember a week in his life when he had missed Sunday School.

That morning Brother Lowry preached on heaven and hell. Oz cried all the way home. "I know I'm a sinner, and I'm lost!" he sobbed.

The next Sunday when everybody stood up to sing the invitation hymn, Oz left his seat and walked to the front. But an older boy walked down the aisle at the same time. Maybe Brother Lowry thought Oz had just tagged along. He didn't even ask the slender fourth grader why he had come forward.

Oz was determined to let everybody know he was trusting Christ as his Lord and Savior. The next Sunday he tried again. This time Brother Lowry received him.

"We're having the baptism out at the slough, Oz," said Brother Lowry. "Are you afraid of water?"

"Oh, no, Sir!" Oz shook his head. "We boys go swimming there all the time."

The slough was a swampy pond backed up from the Crooked River, not far from where it emptied into the big muddy Missouri River. And there, as the church members stood watching on the bank, Oz Quick came up from the water, his curly hair dripping, after being baptized by his pastor.

"Get up, Oz!"

Oz yawned. "What for? It's barely daylight."

His big brother, J. C., shook his shoulder. "Come on, get a move on! Dad told us to be at the grain elevator by six."

6

Still yawning, Oz pulled on his overalls. He stumbled down the stairs to eat breakfast.

"Say, did you see the paper?" J. C. asked him.

"Uh-uh."

"Lindbergh made it—all the way from New York to Paris, France!"

Oz's eyes opened wider. "Is he the same one who used to fly the mail from St. Louis to Chicago?"

J. C. nodded. "Took him over thirty-three hours, but he made it—all the way across the Atlantic, all by himself."

Several times that day Oz wished he were flying, instead of working at Dad's grain elevator. Wagon after wagon would creak down the street. Horses would pull them up onto a slanting wooden platform. Then J. C., Oz, and a hired man would jump onto the wagon sides. Every golden grain of wheat had to be dumped off the back before the team got frisky.

"Watch out, Oz, they're about to bolt!" yelled J. C.

J. C. and the hired man jumped free. But Oz hung on like a monkey in a tree. The farmer yanked on the reins till he finally got his horses under control again and brought them around for another try at unloading.

Later, Oz and the others stood knee-deep in wheat inside a big boxcar under Dad's grain chute. Every corner of the boxcar had to be filled, and that meant fifteen hundred bushels.

Oz tied a red bandana handkerchief over his nose and mouth. Dust got in his eyes, his hair, his overalls.

"Rest awhile, Oz," J. C. told him. "Don't wear yourself out too fast. After all, this is the first summer you've been big enough to handle a scoop."

But the wiry going-on-twelve-year-old kept working. No big brother was going to outdo him now!

When Oz got home at ten that night, he was so sweaty

and filthy that he undressed outdoors and sprayed himself down with the garden hose. Next morning he groaned as sore muscles moved. But by six, he was working at the grain elevator again.

That was the pattern of school holidays for Oz. It began in the summer of 1927 and went on for the next ten years.

Little by little there were more trucks and fewer wagons to unload. But the work was just as hard, whether Oz was scooping wheat or corn, oats or soybeans.

Working for Dad's business could be dangerous. The real "grain elevator" in the place was a long conveyor belt with big buckets that scooped grain from the dump below and hauled it up to the storage bins above. Sometimes, instead of rolling smoothly, the conveyor belt would begin to shake and shudder and slow down. That meant Oz had to crawl underneath and work loose whatever was choking things up.

"Careful, Oz!" J. C. warned him. "That's a good way to break an arm."

Another time it was Oz's leg that nearly got broken. When a freight car was gradually filling with grain from the chute, the boys had to nail big boards across its open side door. Each board was half again as long as Oz and weighed seventy-five pounds. Once a whole stack of grain boards toppled over his knee and foot. It took a week for his sprain to heal. Oz thanked God for keeping him safe from something worse.

J. C. had started working at the elevator years before Oz did. Later their younger brother Dick joined them.

"One good thing about this," Dick panted one day.

"What's that?" asked Oz, stopping a minute to lean on his scoop.

"Working here builds muscles!"

It did. Oz found that out when their new pastor Brother Hurst took groups of boys hiking and camping. Oz could hold his own with any of the other fellows. When it came time for football, basketball, baseball, or track, Oz could hit hard, throw hard, and run hard.

One day Oz found another good thing about working at the grain elevator. Dad had to leave for awhile. On his way out, he told Oz how much to pay if a farmer brought in some corn that day.

Sure enough, a farmer came while Dad was gone. Oz told him what the price would be.

"Oh, come on, Oz!" the man bargained. "Surely you can give me a penny a bushel more than that."

Oz shook his head. "You know how my dad is, don't you, Mr. Crowe? He told me how much it's supposed to be."

The farmer laughed and nodded. Everybody in Hardin, Missouri, knew how honest Deacon John Quick was.

Oz's father believed in education. That was why he had moved to Hardin from Dalton, where Oz was born. He wanted all of his sons and daughters to go to good schools.

During Oz's years in junior high and high school, he kept on developing his muscles as well as his brains. He practiced throwing the shot put for track and field meets. Since he didn't have a heavy metal ball at home, he hoisted a brick instead. But when the brick landed on his head, he decided he'd better try the broad jump.

When Oz was a senior, Hardin High School won every football game. No other team even scored on them. Tight end Oz Quick became a hero one autumn weekend, when he caught a fifty-five yard touchdown pass.

"What do you want to be when you grow up?" people often asked him.

"I want to be a missionary," Oz would say. That had been his answer ever since he had learned in church what a missionary was.

Oz talked with Brother Hurst about it. "Missionaries are mostly preachers or teachers or doctors," Brother Hurst told him. "And a preacher needs to go on to college and seminary."

"Then that's what I've got to do," Oz said to himself. "But it'll take money."

He got a job taking tickets at the theater on Saturdays so he wouldn't have to pay to watch the latest silent movie serial. And when business was slow at Dad's grain elevator, Oz plowed corn for farmers at a dollar a day.

In September 1933, Oz was licensed to preach by his home church. That same month, he moved thirty-five miles west of Hardin to Liberty, Missouri.

William Jewell College stands high on a hill. Since 1849 students had been climbing that hill to study. Oz remembered visiting when his big sister Sallie had been a student. Now it was his turn.

Money was scarce in those Depression days. Oz had only one Sunday suit to last him through four years at William Jewell. He asked for work on campus.

His first job was cleaning Jewell Hall, oldest of the college buildings. It had been a military hospital during the Civil War. Its floors creaked; its woodwork was dark and gloomy.

Oz and his friends liked to stay up late in the dormitory telling ghost stories. "Say, did you hear about that student who used to be janitor at Jewell Hall?" somebody said. "He killed himself in Kansas City last night!"

The shocking news was true. Later, on his way to work Oz glanced at a nearby graveyard. Old Jewell Hall seemed emptier and spookier than ever.

Oz was glad when they changed his job to an auditorium and office building across the way. Every school day he had to get up early and mop any floors he hadn't finished the afternoon before. All day Saturday he had to wash windows, empty wastebaskets, dust furniture, and clean toilets. "A missionary must be willing to work hard," Oz decided.

Fun times came when Oz could go home to Hardin. Mom never knew for sure how many of her seven children would come in late from college or work or dates. So she would just stick her head into the boys' bedroom on one side upstairs, then into the girls' bedroom on the other side. And she would sing out, "How many for breakfast this morning?"

Once Oz came home when Hardin held a basketball tournament. Any team could play. Oz hurried to get his college roommate and several other friends together. They called themselves "The Dorm Rats." And they swept the hometown tournament.

At Second Baptist Church in Liberty, Oz's pastor was Dr. George Sadler. He had been a missionary in Africa. Oz listened to Dr. Sadler's sermons about missions. Oz wondered whether God wanted him to go to Africa.

In 1937 Oz graduated from William Jewell College. That summer he traveled to Nashville, Tennessee. There he learned how to sell Bibles. He was sent with a teammate to mining camps in the mountains of Tennessee, Kentucky, and Virginia. Sometimes the two young men would trudge steep paths all day long without finding a single person who wanted to buy a Bible.

"A missionary must meet many people," Oz decided. "Not everybody you meet will want to hear about God's Word."

At summer's end Oz moved to Louisville, Kentucky. He liked studying at The Southern Baptist Theological Seminary. It was easy to see how courses there could help him become a better missionary.

His job on campus now was waiting on waiters! Oz served the tables where dining hall workers ate before they served all the others.

He found work off campus, too, at Highland Park Baptist Church. "Our auditorium is too small," church members told him. "Oz, why don't you start a separate worship service for boys and girls? This could be in another part of the building."

Oz did. He also rode his bicycle across the big city of Louisville, making visits for the church.

In early 1940, an important guest visited the seminary campus. He was Dr. M. T. Rankin, who had charge of all Southern Baptist missionaries in Asia. Oz and other mission volunteers welcomed Dr. Rankin to a special meeting.

"Why haven't you contacted the Foreign Mission Board, Oz?" Dr. Rankin asked him.

Oz grinned. "Dr. Rankin, I know I want to be a missionary. What I don't know is whether God wants me to be one."

Dr. Rankin nodded. "If you were sure about it, where would you like to go?"

"Maybe Japan," Oz answered. "There's a Japanese student here on campus, you know."

Dr. Rankin smiled. "Maybe God needs you in Japan,

Oz. We only have thirteen missionaries there."

After that, things happened fast. In April of 1940, Oz traveled to Richmond, Virginia. There he was appointed as a foreign missionary. Back in Louisville again, he was ordained a preacher of the gospel. Dad and Mom, his youngest sister, Pauline, and his college roommate, drove all the way from Missouri to see Oz graduate from seminary.

By this time Oz had a girl friend. She and her family were members of Highland Park Church in Louisville.

"Will you come out to Japan and help me, after you finish college and seminary?" Oz asked her.

"To Japan!" the girl's father exploded. "Why, I wouldn't even go there myself!"

But Oz and the girl were still friends. She and her parents offered Oz a ride in their car to California. There Oz would board a passenger ship, leaving San Francisco for Tokyo.

On August 3, 1940, Oz Quick said his good-byes and sailed toward Japan. An older missionary couple on board teased Oz. "At least we'll teach you how to use chopsticks before you land!"

Four Singing Sisters

In Carrollton, Missouri, on a hill twenty miles east of where Oz Quick was growing up in Hardin, there lived four singing sisters.

Mary Evelyn Jones always said she, Dorothy, Bennie, and Clara learned to sing while washing the dishes. In 1933 washing the dishes meant heating water on the stove, filling heavy pans in the sink, and scrubbing and rinsing by hand every dish.

Doing dirty dishes for a family of ten gave plenty of time to sing. Dorothy was the real musician of the four. She could make beautiful sounds come out of their old piano and sing a clear melody as well. Little Clara sang second soprano. Fourteen-year-old Mary Evelyn sang alto. Bennie chimed in wherever her voice was needed.

"Hurry, girls," Bennie urged. "Let's get these dishes done. Then we can hear the man read poetry on the radio in a few minutes."

"But we still have the napkins and sheets and pillow-cases to iron," Mary Evelyn objected.

"And Kenny's starched shirts," added little Clara.

Dorothy placed a stack of plates in the dishpan. "Ironing doesn't make the clatter this does, now, does it? We can iron and listen to the radio at the same time. Come on,

girls, let's sing to make the work go faster!"

Mary Evelyn felt she had a lot to sing about. She remembered first hearing the plan of salvation from her own mother in Sunday School. She remembered walking home from church that Sunday when she was eight, the happiest little girl in Carrollton because she had given her life to the Lord Jesus. She remembered when she was a sixth grader and asked the Holy Spirit to take fuller control of her life.

After that had come the hard times. Her church and her preacher didn't get along. For three years the Jones sisters and their mother had gone to Bible study and worship services at the home of Brother Woodson, who had been the preacher at the church. All the way through junior high school, Mary Evelyn never missed prayer meeting a single time.

Finally things had straightened out again. Now they were all happy to be back in church. Mary Evelyn tried to learn a new piano piece every week, so she could play it on Sunday night. Shy as she was, she also began to take speaking parts on programs at church.

Everybody loved to hear the four sisters sing. A lawyer in town even invited them to present a banquet program for his civic club. So the girls began practicing Stephen Foster's songs, as well as hymns for church.

The singing stopped for awhile when Mary Evelyn was a junior in high school. Dad worked hard at his grocery store, from seven in the morning till six o'clock at night. Mom helped, especially all day on Saturdays. But the middle 1930s were hard times all over America. When Mary's father got sick, he had to close his store.

Big sister Irene and big brothers Harry and George came

home to talk over the family crisis. Kenny got a job in somebody else's grocery, and his wages paid the house rent. Bennie went to work as a dental assistant.

Everybody was surprised when the owner of a dry goods store came to see Mom. "How about Mary Evelyn working for me this summer?" he asked.

Mary Evelyn felt she would never have been brave enough to go out and get a job on her own. But she enjoyed unrolling smooth bolts of cloth and answering customers' questions. The store owner liked her work. When school started again in September, Mary Evelyn kept on working after classes and on Saturdays.

After graduating from high school, Mary Evelyn stayed on at the dry goods store. "I wish I could go to college, like George did," she said to herself. "But how?"

For three years she worked and saved her money. A boy-friend in town began to get serious. He planned to go to the University of Missouri in Columbia. Mary Evelyn hoped one day she could do that too.

The four singing sisters were as popular as ever. One summer day in 1940, they were invited to sing for a special service at Hardin Baptist Church.

"We're sending one of our young men as a missionary," the Hardin church members explained.

Mary Evelyn turned to her sisters. "We've never even had a missionary to speak at our church, have we?"

Dorothy and Bennie and Clara all shook their heads.

Mary saw Oz Quick that summer day, along with his parents and brothers and sisters. She saw the fine Bible and portable typewriter being given to help him in his work. When the service was over, she went back home to Carrollton.

That was a busy summer. Mary Evelyn's dreams were about to come true. In September 1940, she moved to a dormitory on campus and enrolled as a freshman at the University of Missouri.

"Name, please?" they asked her when she signed up for her classes.

"Mary Jones," she answered. She never had liked *Evelyn* as part of her name. Now was her chance to get rid of it.

During that school year, the war news on the radio got worse and worse. America began building factories to make ships, planes, and tanks for its allies fighting in Europe.

Big sister Irene and her husband moved to Long Beach, California. "There are a lot of jobs out here, Dad," they wrote back home to Carrollton. "Why don't you move in with us and try to find work?"

Mary's father was feeling stronger. In 1941 he did move to California. Soon he was working at a big shipbuilding plant. He wrote for the family to join him.

Mary Jones had used up most of her savings during just one year in college. When the family moved, she moved with them. But by now she was wearing an engagement ring to help her remember a certain young man at the University of Missouri.

Holidays and Hard Times

Oz Quick never forgot New Year's Day 1941. Not January 1, but the lunar new year, celebrated in February by the Japanese. Tens of thousands of people crowded around the imperial palace in Tokyo. They waved lanterns and shouted "Banzai! Banzai!" [BON-sigh.] They were cheering for the emperor, wishing him ten thousand years more of life and victory.

War was evident in Asia. Day by day Oz saw small flat boxes that held the ashes of Japanese soldiers being brought back for burial. He wasn't surprised, soon after the lunar new year, when he was told to ship out.

All missionaries still studying language in Japan had to leave. Some went home to America. But Oz and four others talked Dr. Rankin into letting them shift over to China, Japan's enemy in the war.

Two weeks before Easter, Oz landed at Kweilin [gway-LINN], in Free China. First he had sailed from Tokyo to Shanghai, next from Shanghai to Hong Kong. Then he had flown by night over battle lines.

Flares lighted the runway as the twin-motor DC-3 glided down through drizzling rain. Older missionaries in Kweilin were glad to greet Oz. Even though he couldn't speak Chinese, there was a lot a lively young man could do.

Refugees were pouring into Kweilin from war zones to the east. Many of them were college students who knew some English. Oz began teaching English Bible classes. Every night he helped lead evangelistic services. Almost every night, people stayed afterward to learn more about the gospel, the good news. Chinese church members among the refugees helped the missionaries hold inquirers' classes.

People who attended services in Kweilin were noisy and restless—not at all like the quiet Japanese Christians Oz had met at the small churches in Tokyo. "In America, people's minds wander during church," Oz remarked one day. "In China, their whole bodies wander!"

When air-raid sirens sounded, everybody had to get up and leave. "Come on, Oz, to the caves!" the other missionaries yelled the first day Oz heard that long high-pitched wail over a loudspeaker.

Oz blinked at the size of limestone caves in hillsides near Kweilin. One of them could hold two thousand people. "Were these dug for bomb shelters?" he asked.

"No, but they work, don't they?" came the answer.

Usually the Japanese bombers raided during daylight hours. Sometimes Oz and the others spent all morning in a cave; sometimes it was all day. That got long for missionary kids (MKs) in the group. The MKs were three-year-old Ralph, four-year-old Carolyn, five-year-old Dorothy, seven-year-old Howard, and nine-year-old George. Oz helped by singing with the children and telling them funny stories.

There was plenty to do when air raids and Bible classes and church services and language study left any time to do it. Oz lived in a huge, old eight-room barn of a house that had been empty for two years. He and a Chinese hired man swept, picked broken glass out of window frames, nailed

together shutters that banged in the wind, painted wood-work, and repaired fences. Oz shared his house with two dogs, two canaries, a cat, and too many mosquitoes to count.

On Thanksgiving Day of 1941, Oz felt he had a lot to be thankful for. None of the missionaries had been hurt by bombs. Hard times had caused many Chinese to turn to the Lord Jesus.

Oz was thankful for good food. After eight months of mostly eating by himself, he was glad to start sharing meals with Miss Hattie Stallings. Miss Stallings had been in China longer than any of the other missionaries. On Thanksgiving Day they all gathered at her house to help her celebrate twenty-five years of telling the good news in villages near Kweilin.

But that delicious roast goose with all the trimmings didn't seem to agree with Oz Quick. Or maybe the ache in his side started after his long hike into the country on Friday. Or maybe it was that Sunday dinner with Chinese friends.

Whatever caused it, Miss Stallings put Oz to bed on a liquid diet. Two doctors checked him over.

"Seems like appendicitis to me," said Dr. Bacon.

Dr. Beddoe looked solemn. "One of our missionaries died of appendicitis, just a year ago."

"We're not set up to operate on him here, with the air raids and all," said Dr. Bacon.

"And to get him to my hospital," added Dr. Beddoe, "he'd have to travel five days by riverboat."

So they decided to send Oz out again over the battle lines to Hong Kong. In that British colony, there was no fighting.

The plane flew only once a week. Usually it took ten

days to get a ticket. But Oz was sick, and that speeded things up. After a day's delay, the DC-3 taxied up to the bamboo-mat shed which was the waiting room. An older missionary helped Oz aboard. Through light rain Oz saw mountains, rice fields, and a big river. Then the plane landed in Hong Kong.

The next day Dr. Rankin helped Oz buy pajamas, toothpaste, and shaving cream. In the afternoon he took Oz to Matilda Hospital, high on a hill across the harbor.

The doctor's secretary was a young black man from Jamaica. He and a Scottish nurse helped Oz move into the men's ward.

There were ten patients in the room. Oz soon learned that one of them talked and whistled in his sleep. Then for awhile he didn't think about much except how sick he felt because Dr. Montgomery put him to sleep and took out his appendix.

Dr. Rankin and two missionary friends came to see Oz on Saturday, December 6. They brought him flowers. He wanted to laugh when Dr. Rankin said something funny, but that hurt his stitches too much.

Each evening the men in the ward listened to the news on the radio. That Saturday, reserve troops began to be called out in Hong Kong. By Sunday they were calling for volunteers to drive ambulances.

Dr. Montgomery preached a good sermon on Sunday morning. After lights went out that night, Oz heard big guns going off. "That's artillery practice over at Stanley Fortress," one of the men explained.

On Monday morning there were more explosions. "It's just the cannons at Stanley again," said the men.

Oz shook his head. "I've heard bombs before, fellows. That's not cannon fire."

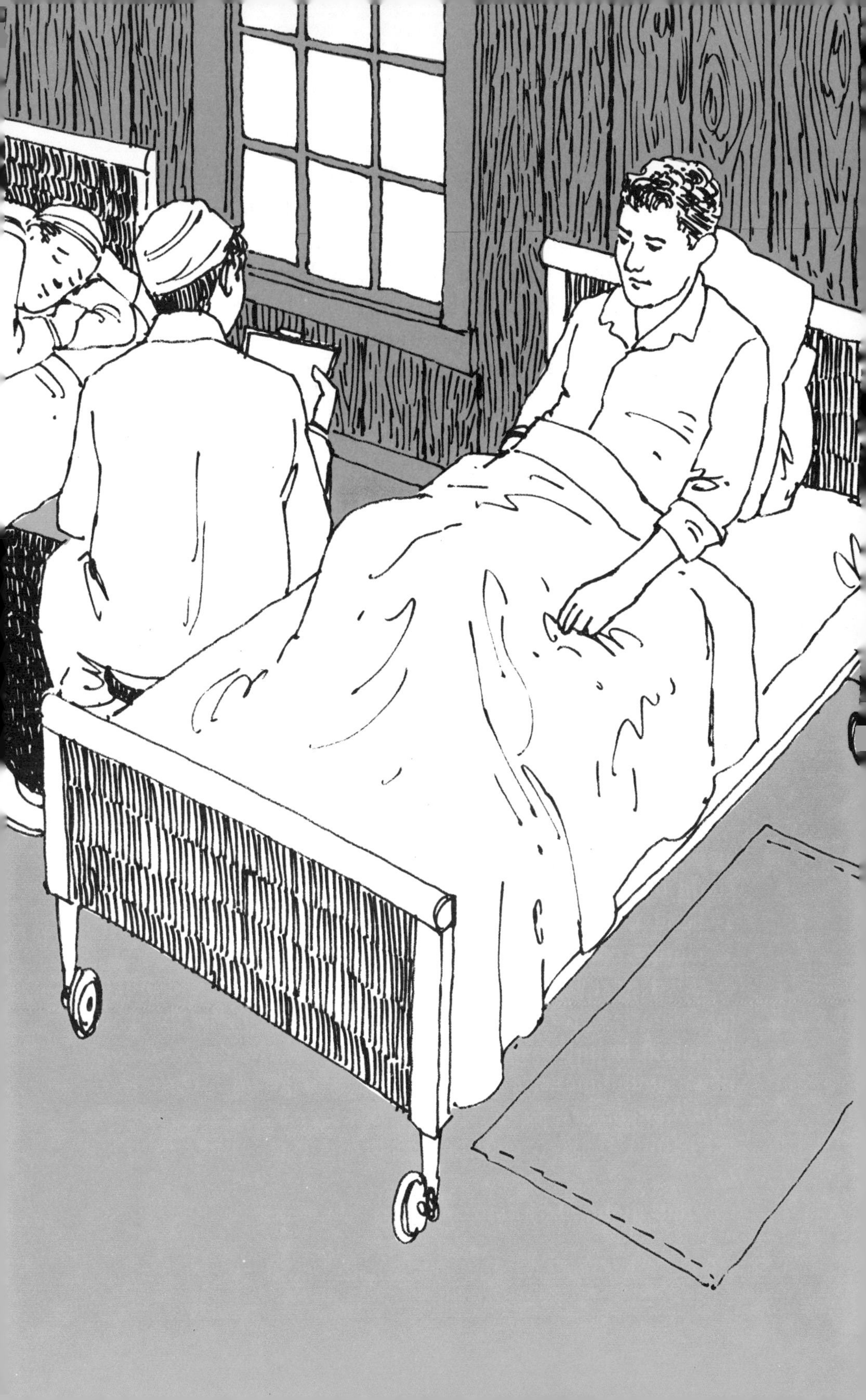

At nine o'clock a nurse walked into the men's ward. "Japan has declared war," she announced. Oz felt as if the bottom of his stomach had dropped out.

All patients who could possibly walk were sent home. But Oz was stuck. Late that afternoon, he heard the too-familiar sound of an air-raid warning.

The next day sirens started right after breakfast. About a hundred and fifty yards from the hospital, Hong Kong soldiers answered with machine gun fire. This brought more Japanese planes—six waves of them that day.

Dr. Rankin came across by ferry. He brought Oz his overcoat and other things he had left behind. Then Japanese troops captured the harbor, and Dr. Rankin's own things had to be left behind.

Oz's stitches came out the day Hong Kong's harbor and airport fell to the enemy. The next day, dozens of women and children crowded into Matilda Hospital. The day after that, Oz and everybody else moved down to the basement for safety. For the next two weeks, he slept on a long wicker deck chair.

By the middle of December, Oz was up and walking again. That was a good thing because now the Japanese could turn shore batteries toward the hills. Shells, as well as bombs, began hitting all around the hospital.

Things got no better by a week before Christmas. Oz decided he'd better try to find Dr. Rankin and the other missionaries on Hong Kong Island. After that, he thought he might help the soldiers by volunteering to drive one of those ambulances. So Oz packed his bag and reported to Dr. Montgomery.

"I think maybe you'd better stay here a few more days, Oz," said Dr. Montgomery.

That night Oz found out why: Japanese soldiers had

already landed in the port at the foot of the hill.

Dr. Montgomery gave Oz a Red Cross armband and put him to work. First he tore up anti-Japanese propaganda leaflets, hospital records, and anything else that might make trouble if they were captured.

On December 20, the hospital's electricity was cut off. So was its water. Oz and the young Jamaican secretary dodged whistling shells outside the main gate to pull up buckets of water from a well thirty feet deep. They cleaned smoky lamp chimneys. They carried patients who were too sick to move by themselves.

By now the hospital buildings had taken several direct hits. The worst was a shell that blasted all the way through the baby ward. But it was a dud, and no one was hurt.

Dr. Montgomery said, "Oz, the operating room windows have already been blown out by explosions. But if you could open the other windows upstairs, maybe we could save some of our plate glass."

Oz tried. Every time a Japanese bomber dived, Oz dived for cover too. After several rounds of "You dive, I dive," he finally got all the windows open. Then Oz yelled at the sky, "You dive, I quit!" and ran back downstairs.

On Christmas Day, Oz and his Jamaican friend decided to celebrate by taking their first bath in two weeks. Water was precious, but they managed to sneak off with two buckets of it.

Oz was using every drop of the dirty bathwater by rinsing out his underwear, when his friend came in. He had a strange look on his face. "Hong Kong has surrendered to the Japanese," he said.

Oz didn't believe him at first. But it was true. The bombing and shelling stopped. Gradually everybody moved back upstairs. Oz helped sweep up dust and broken glass. It felt good to sleep in a bed again.

On December 27, the Japanese ordered everybody out of Matilda Hospital. But Dr. Montgomery talked them into waiting a few more weeks.

Oz celebrated the new year of 1942 by hiking down to see his missionary friends in the port area below. It was more than a thousand steps down steep slopes beside the tramway tracks. But Oz knew he needed to go because of Dr. Rankin's letter: Armed robbers had taken the missionaries' watches, rings, and money!

There was only one other man besides Dr. Rankin in the little group of missionaires. With looters all around, one man needed to stay on guard at home, while two men scouted for supplies.

Oz and Dr. Rankin walked miles that day. They were looking for chocolate, corn, tomatoes, oatmeal, raisins, matches—all the things they could usually buy in stores. But now all the stores were boarded shut. They had to pay sky-high prices to hawkers along the street.

Once a Japanese sentry stopped Dr. Rankin. Then he saw Oz's Red Cross armband and let them go ahead.

Oz was nearly worn out when they got back to the missionaries' home with their heavy loads. And there on the bridge, just across the tramway, a gang of thirty looters stood watching them!

Not one looter made a move as Oz and Dr. Rankin scurried past. Later, one man tried to climb the steps. Oz and Dr. Rankin threatened him with bricks and iron pipes. He left.

It was after dark when Oz started his weary climb up the hill beside the tramway again. A full moon shone just as his Jamaican friend made a last nighttime checkup. He unlocked the front gate of the hospital to let Oz in.

The next time Oz hiked down to town, the other missionaries were gone. The Japanese had herded them off to prison. Oz and Chinese Christians managed to buy tin cups and plates and other things they needed.

Another hospital near Matilda was closed by the Japanese on January 22. Oz picked up some food, medicine, and vitamins from the other hospital's supplies. He was glad he did because just two days later he was imprisoned.

First the prisoners were moved by trucks down mountain roads to the harbor. Then they traveled two hours by boat around the end of Hong Kong Island to Stanley.

Oz was lucky: Dr. Rankin heard he had come and managed to get him as a roommate. They and four other men had cots, chairs, a table, and a cabinet. Some of the prisoners had to sleep on bare concrete floors.

"We're beginning to get hungry here, Oz," Dr. Rankin told him. "What kind of food did you bring us?"

Dr. Rankin's smile faded when Oz showed him a gallon of cod-liver oil and two bags of vitamin pills.

The prison camp was actually a complex of apartment buildings for prison wardens and their families. Like William Jewell College, it sat high on a hill. Three thousand people were crowded behind barbed wire barricades. From three sides, Oz could see the ocean far below.

Many of the prisoners were boys and girls, captured along with their parents. Oz remembered his days at Highland Park Baptist Church in Louisville. Soon he was holding children's services every Sunday. He began pitching for a softball team too.

But it wasn't long before the games stopped. Food was scarce. So was clean, boiled drinking water. Dr. Rankin and the rest decided Oz had been smart after all to bring vitamins and cod-liver oil. Still, Oz lost twenty pounds between January and April.

Things got a little better in the spring. The Japanese added flour to prison rations. Dr. Rankin turned out to be a good bread baker. Sometimes Chinese friends risked their lives to send the missionaries packages of food.

Oz never forgot the Fourth of July 1942. By that time he and the others were aboard a Portuguese ship. They were on their way to be exchanged for Japanese prisoners of war. On July 4 the ship rode at anchor near Saigon. And the Japanese let the ship stewards serve an unusually good meal.

Even after that extra food, Oz knew he looked thin. He had shaved off the full beard he had grown at Stanley Prison. His cheeks looked hollow when he glanced in the mirror.

He celebrated his twenty-seventh birthday on the Atlantic Ocean. The long trip home brought him by way of Singapore, Mozambique, and Brazil. Two days after Oz's birthday, on August 25, 1942, the mercy ship docked in the Hudson River at New York City.

Open Doors for Mary

In the summer of 1942, Mary Jones felt miserable. Working in an office at the shipbuilding plant was dull and monotonous. Other workers there did things Mary didn't want to do. They went places Mary didn't want to go.

Even going to church in California didn't mean as much as it used to back home in Missouri. Fifty thousand factory workers had to take turns having time off. Sometimes Mary had to work at night. Sometimes she had to work on Sunday.

One Sunday evening at church, Mary realized she had no goals, no hopes for her life. She came home crying. "Lord, I'll do anything you want me to. Just show me the way!"

Gradually Mary realized God didn't want her to marry that young man in Missouri. So she planned to travel all the way back and return his engagement ring.

In that wartime September, trains bulged with men in uniform. For three days and two nights Mary sat in a crowded coach, all the way from Long Beach to Kansas City.

By now big brother George was a doctor. Mary stayed with George and his wife in Waverly, Missouri. She gave the ring back to the young man at the university, and that was that.

"While I'm here, I might as well visit some other kin-folk," she said. So Mary traveled to her hometown to see her aunt.

"She's not here, Mary," the neighbors said. "She went to church for some kind of meeting."

Mary slipped into the old familiar church in Carrollton and sat down at the back. A young man stood talking to Baptist women gathered from towns and villages all around. He looked thin and weak. Yet his eyes twinkled as he told about his adventures in Asia.

After the meeting, the women introduced Mary Jones to Oz Quick.

"Oh, I remember you," he said. "Didn't you and your sisters sing when I left Hardin for Japan two years ago?"

"That's right."

Oz smiled. "How about walking to town with me for a soft drink?"

As they sipped their soft drinks through straws, Oz began telling Mary about Japan. "It's a beautiful country. Tokyo is quiet, clean, full of hard-working people who don't try to steal your things like they do in China."

"Are there already some Christians in Japan?" Mary asked him.

"Yes, but not many. The few churches are small. You feel like Moses when you go to church there."

"Oh? Why's that?" Mary wondered.

Oz chuckled. "Moses took off his shoes before the burning bush, didn't he? Well, you have to take off your shoes to go to church in Japan. In winter, you think your feet are going to freeze!"

They laughed together. Then it was Mary's turn to talk. She told Oz about her dreams of going on to college.

"Why don't you go to William Jewell?" he asked.

Soda 5¢

Mary frowned. "Isn't it sort of expensive?"

Oz stood up to pay for their drinks. "Let's go over and find out. I'll see if I can borrow Dad's car tomorrow. OK?"

That night at George's home, Mary talked to God a long time. In her prayer she wondered, "Lord, is this a door you are opening in my life?"

The next day Mary saw William Jewell College for the first time in her life. Oz introduced her to the interim president of the college. Dr. Hester asked her many questions. Finally he said, "Mary, you'll be two weeks late starting, but I'm sure you can catch up. And I'm sure you can find enough work to pay your way through college."

The day after that, Oz took Mary home to Hardin. Three of his sisters greeted her. Mary wondered why teenage Pauline giggled when Oz got out his souvenirs and found that Mary could wear a pair of fancy Japanese shoes. "Don't you remember that story about Cinderella and the slippers, Mary?" Pauline teased her.

After that, Mary had to hurry. She made the long train trip to California again so she could pack her clothes for college. A letter from Oz was waiting for her there. As soon as she knew when she could get another ticket, Mary answered his letter. And Oz was waiting at the station when Mary finally got back to Kansas City.

Then Mary settled down to work. Dr. Hester was right. She soon caught up with all her classes. And typing letters and averaging grades in the college registrar's office helped pay her bills.

Oz turned up in November at a Baptist student convention in Columbia. He and Mary sat together. Yet somehow they didn't feel as close as they had before.

Oz stayed busy traveling around to speak about missions. Sometimes he remembered to write; sometimes he didn't. Mary stayed busy at college. She even started dating one of the few boys who hadn't left the campus to join the Army, Navy, Air Force, or Marines.

Liberty, Missouri, was hot in the summer of 1943. But Mary stayed on the job. She took summer classes and made thirty-five cents an hour working in the registrar's office. By September she was a junior in college. Her youngest sister, Clara, was a freshman that year.

That month Oz Quick dropped by again. "I'm getting tired of just talking about missions, Mary," he confessed. "Looks like I can't go back and preach in China or Japan anytime soon, with the war still going on. So maybe I'll become an Army chaplain."

Sure enough, Oz wore a uniform the next time Mary saw him. It was just before Christmas. He was on his way to chaplains' training in faraway Massachusetts.

"My, you look handsome!" said Mary.

That was the last Mary saw or heard of Oz till just a week before final exams in May. One Sunday afternoon he phoned her from Hardin. "May I come over this evening?" he asked.

Wartime gasoline rationing made it hard to drive a car out of town. But Oz had somehow managed to get enough gas. He drove his dad's '38 Plymouth up the hill to the campus. He looked handsomer than ever.

"I have a special ten-day leave, Mary," he explained. "We're stationed way out in Oregon, and we may be leaving for the Pacific war zone any day now." Then he took a deep breath and looked her straight in the eye. "I think we ought to get married."

Mary gasped. "Now? This week? How . . . why?"

Oz looked solemn. "If we don't get married now, Mary, we may never get married."

She sat silent a moment. Everybody knew at least one man or boy who had died in battle.

Mary talked with her brother George and his wife. She talked with Dr. Hester at college. She talked with the registrar, her boss. Everybody said, "If you want to marry him, Mary, then go ahead."

Just two weeks before, she had bought a navy blue suit. It was her first new outfit since starting back to college. It could be her wedding dress.

"But Missouri law says you're supposed to wait three days before getting married!" Mary suddenly realized. Then she remembered the lawyer who used to invite four singing sisters to banquets for his civic club. The lawyer was a judge now. He worked things out so Mary and Oz wouldn't have to wait.

On Mother's Day, May 14, 1944, Oz preached at his home church in Hardin. He invited everybody to the wedding. Over at Second Baptist Church in Liberty, Dr. Cutts gave the same invitation. The church was full that afternoon to see Oz and Mary get married.

The next day Oz had to leave for Atlanta, Georgia. He was scheduled to attend the annual Southern Baptist Convention as a chaplains' representative. That same Monday, Mary had to begin her final exams.

During the next three months, Oz and Mary managed to spend a total of twenty-eight days together. Part of those days were in Missouri. Others were in Oregon and in California. When the 96th Infantry Division shipped out, Mary came home for her senior year of college.

Sometimes weeks would pass without Mary receiving even one letter from Oz. Then several would come on the same day. Most had words and whole sentences scissored out. Mary knew that military censors had to check on anything that might be picked up by enemy spies.

"I took care of a little girl last night," one of Oz's letters began. He went on to tell Mary about a mother on Okinawa

who strayed into the line of fire and about a little two-year-old left an orphan. Chaplain Quick got her quiet and put her to bed in his foxhole.

Another time Oz wrote a letter for a wounded soldier. The boy's father ran a jewelry store in Kansas City. He found out that Mary had no engagement ring. Before long, Mary was wearing a diamond that matched the plain wedding band Oz had given her that day in May.

After graduating from college in the spring of 1945, Mary moved closer to Oz for awhile. She became a summer student home missionary. Leading camps and Vacation Bible Schools in northern California felt nearer to mission work in Asia than typing term papers and report cards in Liberty, Missouri.

Mary never knew exactly where Oz was. She listened to the radio, read the papers, and tried to figure out where the 96th Infantry might be stationed. And she thanked God when the war ended suddenly at the end of summer.

In the fall, Mary started to seminary at Louisville, Kentucky. She ran into a problem on campus: "No married women may live in the dormitory."

"But—but—my husband isn't even here!" Mary argued.

"Sorry, no wives—only single women."

So every day Mary had to walk down one steep hill and up another to a rented room near the campus. That was where Oz found her when he finally came home from the Army with special citations for heroic service under fire. It was early spring, 1946.

That April Oz and Mary traveled together to Richmond, Virginia. It was exactly six years since Oz Quick had first been appointed a foreign missionary. Now Mary Quick was appointed to become his missionary teammate.

More Open Doors

During the war years Oz had seen how useful an airplane could be in Asia. In the summer of 1946, he and Mary moved to Toccoa, Georgia, where missionaries could learn to fly.

They planned to take flying lessons together. But Mary was grounded at first.

All flight students had to take a physical examination. Dr. Ayers was another missionary waiting to get back into China. He checked Mary over.

"I'm sorry," he said, "I can't clear you for flight training with those bad tonsils." So Mary's tonsillectomy delayed her flying lessons by a month.

That fall, the Foreign Mission Board sent Oz and Mary Quick to Yale University in New Haven, Connecticut. "Study Chinese there, while we wait to see what opens up," they were told.

Oz's friend Dr. Rankin came to New England for a visit. He now had charge of Southern Baptist missionaries all over the world. "How would you like to go to Manchuria?" he asked.

Manchuria had once been part of China, but Japan had taken it over. "It's cold there," Dr. Rankin warned them. Oz and Mary made the rounds of army outlet stores, buying woolen clothes and long underwear.

After a year of language study, the Quicks at last started toward Asia again in the summer of 1947. They couldn't get permission to take a plane into Manchuria, so Oz never used his pilot's license.

On the West Coast a telegram from Richmond caught up with them: "One of our missionaries in Kweilin is sick. Would you pray about going there to help out?"

"Kweilin?" Oz grinned. "Why, that would be like going back home!"

A converted troop carrier doesn't make the most comfortable ship for crossing the Pacific. Mary shared a cabin with twenty-four women and two babies. Oz had to sleep with a roomful of men. The sea was rough nearly all the way across.

In Hong Kong, Mary took her first ride in a Chinese pedicab. She spent her first night in a rundown Chinese hotel. Their room had no window curtains. They woke up the next morning to find curious Chinese peeking in from an apartment across the narrow street.

Mary got to Kweilin before Oz did. He had to travel the long way by boat, bringing the baggage. Mary flew in, as Oz had done that first time in 1941.

While waiting for Oz, Mary stayed with two women missionaries. Weeds grew waist-high in their yard. "Watch your step, Mary," one of them warned her. "We do have cobras, you know."

There was no running water and no electricity in the missionaries' home. Mary had to learn to bathe from a bucket. She didn't like the big Chinese spiders, either. They made even bigger shadows by lamplight.

One day Mary noticed a door that looked chewed around

40

the edges. "What happened here?" she asked.

"Oh, just rats, trying to get in the attic to eat up our salaries," the missionaries explained.

Mary learned that Chinese money was becoming more worthless every day. As fast as the missionaries' pay got to Kweilin, they hurried to buy big bags of rice because rice kept its value. The rats were after that rice in the attic.

Mary's first worship services in Chinese were with the missionaries' household helpers. One of the women asked Mary to quote John 3:16. She couldn't. After that, she tried to speed up memorizing Bible verses in Chinese.

When Oz arrived, the church in Kweilin gave the Quicks a reception. Men sat on one side, women on the other. "If I watch Oz and do what he does, I'll be all right," Mary said to herself.

Mary wondered when she saw Oz taking the cookies they were offered along with tea. She had already noticed cookies like that in shops along the street. They didn't look clean. But she took some and ate them. After they got home, she found all of Oz's cookies in his coat pocket!

Home in Kweilin meant two rooms in a bombed-out schoolhouse. The big old house where Oz had lived before had been gutted, like more than 90 percent of Kweilin. Rats, rubble, and weeds filled all the schoolrooms except one upstairs and one downstairs. There Oz and Mary lived. The rooms had no ceilings. One winter night, sleet came through their roof.

Mary began to feel the Lord had given her a hopeless job. She wondered how anybody could come to know Jesus where people were so poor and where everything seemed so confused.

Then one night a young man knocked on the school-house door. "I'm miserable," he said in Chinese. "There's no peace in my heart."

42

Oz read the Bible with him. Mary joined them in prayer. The young man asked Jesus to take charge of his life. Mary realized that the Lord had opened another door and that his power can work anywhere.

A few months later, the Quicks moved into a larger house. Every Saturday, forty young people came to see them. Oz and Mary mostly led in singing because it was still hard for them to use Chinese.

One day a high school teacher invited Mary to give a cake-baking demonstration. She wondered whether she had done the right thing in saying yes. Mary remembered hearing her mother say, "Mary is the only one of my daughters who could ever fail trying to make my never-fail cake icing!"

Mary laid careful plans with Ah Hong, the Chinese man who helped her in the kitchen. She fussed over her tiny woodburning stove.

First she baked one cake at home so there would be enough for each boy and girl in the high school class to have a piece. The cake didn't look like much, but Mary figured it would have to do. Leaving Ah Hong to finish icing it, she hurried off to school.

Chinese students watched eagerly as Mary measured flour, sugar, milk, eggs, and everything else that makes a cake taste good. The stove at school was even smaller than the one at home. It was a charcoal hibachi, with a tiny oven on top.

Mary told a Bible story with pictures while the cake baked. When it was about done, she sent some of the boys by bicycle to bring the other cake from home.

The boys came back wide-eyed, bringing with them the fanciest cake Mary had ever seen! She wondered whether everyone would expect her to make the second cake look as pretty as the first one did.

FLOUR
SUGAR

But the red-and-green cake wasn't the only thing making those schoolboys excited. "Somebody sighted a tiger from the mountains near here!" they warned. "You'd better go right on home."

So Mary never had to ice the second cake. Later she said to Oz, "I had no idea Ah Hong knew how to make such beautiful cake decorations!"

"What did he use to color the icing red and green?" Oz asked.

Mary giggled. "I wouldn't dare ask him."

Church services in Kweilin seemed to take forever. Sermons lasted two hours. Mary soon found out one reason the preacher kept talking so long: people came and went so that the whole congregation (except for the Quicks) might change two or three times before the service was over. But Oz and Mary loved the Chinese Christians, who loved them in return.

Early in 1948, the Quicks knew that their first child was on the way.

"What'll we do?" Mary asked Oz. "The doctor here says she's not set up to deliver a baby."

"I guess you'll have to go out to Hong Kong," said Oz.

Then who should turn up in Kweilin but Dr. Ayers, who had taken out Mary's tonsils two years before. "We're moving Baptist Hospital here to get away from the Communists," he explained. When he saw Mary was going to have a baby, he gladly agreed to take care of her.

Mary Lou Quick was born at night, by lamplight. She was a beautiful baby girl.

But the next day, Mrs. Ayers noticed a tiny pink mark on the baby's cheek. It turned dark red. Another spot showed up, just below her eye. The red marks began to swell and then to grow together. Soon Mary Lou's whole cheek was puffy.

"It's a growing birthmark," Dr. Ayers explained. "I've read about such things in medical books, but I've never seen one before. I'm not even sure what kind of specialist your baby needs."

Oz and Mary looked at each other.

"We need to take Mary Lou to America," said Mary.

"But if we leave China now, the Communists may never let us back in," said Oz.

They prayed. Finally they knew the answer, but it was as hard as the question: Oz must stay, and Mary must go.

Just before Christmas of 1948, Oz took his little family to the seaport of Canton. There they heard of a ship sailing from Shanghai. They flew to Shanghai. Then they found that the naval ship had room for only one person.

"But Mary Lou is just a tiny baby!" they cried.

"Sorry—one berth, one passenger."

Oz had had enough. He marched down to an airline office and reserved plane tickets to Los Angeles for his wife and daughter.

Dr. Cauthen held Dr. Rankin's old job in Asia now. He was Oz's friend. Oz had helped take care of the little Cauthens in the bomb-shelter caves of Kweilin. But no other Southern Baptist missionary had ever tried to fly all the way from Shanghai to America.

"Let's ask one other doctor to check Mary Lou," Dr. Cauthen advised.

Dr. Bryan looked at Mary Lou's once-pretty face. The reddish birthmark had swelled up level with the bridge of her nose. Her eye and mouth were pulled out of shape. "This baby needs to go home—*now*," urged Dr. Bryan.

So Mary and Mary Lou boarded a propeller plane for the

long, long trip. It took eight hours to Guam, another eight to Midway, and another eight to Honolulu. Air pressure in the cabin went up and down when the plane did. Mary thought Mary Lou would never stop crying.

The last lap was the worst of all. It took twelve hours to fly from Honolulu to Los Angeles. Then the airport was fogged in, and the plane had to land in Burbank instead.

Mary staggered down the steps into her mother's arms. "I'm so glad you got word in time to make it to this airport!" she cried.

Missionary doctors in China had wanted Mary to take her baby to Houston, Texas. But Mary's mother had other ideas. "You don't know anybody in Houston," she said.

"And Children's Hospital here is as good as any," Mary's sister Bennie added.

Bennie took Mary and Mary Lou to Children's Hospital in Los Angeles. The hospital receptionist began filling out forms. "What kind of doctor do you need to see?" she asked.

"I don't know," Mary answered.

"Who's your regular doctor here?"

Mary shook her head again. "We just got in two days ago from Shanghai."

"Shanghai!" The woman's face lit up. "I have a brother in the Navy at Shanghai! Have you really lived over there?"

Soon they were chatting like old friends. "Don't you worry about a thing," the receptionist told Mary. "We'll work it all out."

The first doctor said Mary Lou needed to see three specialists. Mary's new friend, the receptionist, made three appointments for her.

The first specialist said, "I can't do a thing about this kind of birthmark. It's grown too deep."

The second specialist had to break his appointment because of an emergency case.

The third specialist said, "Yes, I know exactly what's wrong with Mary Lou. And I know how to cure her too. But it'll take several months. Do you want me to begin the treatment?"

Mary didn't know what to say.

The doctor glanced down at the appointment card in his hand. "Mrs. Quick, I see you're a missionary in China. Is the problem money?"

"Oh, no!" she answered. Mary knew she and Oz had only about ninety dollars in the bank. But she also knew they would somehow find whatever it took to make Mary Lou well again.

The specialist smiled. "I'm a preacher's kid. When I was little, we never had to pay doctor bills. How about if I charge you only what it actually costs to treat your baby?"

Mary felt as if a load had dropped off her shoulders. "Doctor, could you begin today?" she begged.

It took a long time before Mary could see that X-rays and radium treatments were making any difference. Gradually Mary Lou's little face looked normal.

Oz wrote from Kweilin. Strikes had closed the university. Three Christian college students were living with him. Oz didn't know how much longer he could stay in China. But he reminded Mary that all the church members in Kweilin were praying for Mary Lou.

Then one day in the summer of 1949, another letter said, "Meet me in Manila!"

God had opened another door. Now Oz and Mary Quick would become God's missionaries to Chinese people in the Philippines.

Teammates in Taiwan

In the Philippines Oz and Mary Quick and little Mary Lou lived at mile-high Baguio [BOG-ee-yo]. That was where the Chinese language school had moved after Communists took over Peking, the capital city of the mainland.

Every Saturday Oz and other missionaries rode zigzag trails down to hot, steamy Dagupan [dah-GOO-pahn]. There they held Vacation Bible Schools and revival services. They helped Chinese living in Dagupan to start their own Baptist church.

Every Monday after daybreak, the missionaries traveled back up to cool, rainy Baguio. There Mary Lou's little brother, John, was born in July 1950.

Mission work in the Philippines seemed slow and hard. Travel had to be done by daylight because rebels stalked the roadsides. Chinese people in Dagupan spoke a different kind of Chinese from the language Oz and Mary had been learning for so many years in so many places. Even after all that study, the Quicks had to ask interpreters to translate everything they said.

On the way to meet Mary and Mary Lou at Manila in 1949, Oz had stopped first at the island of Taiwan. That was where the government of Free China had moved when Communists won the civil war.

"Why can't we do mission work in Taiwan, Oz?" Mary asked him.

"It still seems too unsettled for families with children to live there," he explained. "But maybe one of these days. . . ."

In February 1951, Oz was invited to Taiwan again. He held revival meetings in several churches. Chinese pastors and six single women missionaries begged him to stay and help them.

Back in Baguio, Oz bubbled with excitement. "People in Taiwan speak the same kind of Chinese we do, Mary!" he told her. "In fact, lots of them have just come over from the mainland."

Only two months later the Quicks moved mission fields one last time. For the next thirty years, Taiwan would be their home.

They stopped in Hong Kong on the way. Their friend Dr. Cauthen said, "You'll need transportation in Taiwan." So Oz bought a motorcycle and took it with them on the boat.

Bertha Smith greeted them at Amoy Street Baptist Chapel in Taipei [tie-BAY]. Miss Bertha was past sixty, but she smiled like a schoolgirl to see people pouring into the little chapel building. "They've left everything behind them," she told Oz and Mary. "Their families, their homes, their idols—everything. And they're hungry to find something to fill the empty places in their lives. I'm so glad you've come to help us tell them what that something is!"

Sunday School classes overflowed Amoy Street Chapel and met outside. Youth meetings and evangelistic services brought crowds too. "All we have to do is open the doors and turn on the lights, and people come!" said Mary.

50

One Sunday in the middle of morning worship a young man yelled, "Who is God? Where is this God you're talking about?"

For once the crowded chapel was quiet. From behind the pulpit, Oz politely answered the young man's questions. And more and more people turned to the God Oz Quick was talking about.

There was no room to put a baptistry inside the chapel. Oz had one built outside. The first time it was used, he baptized twenty-six people.

The next year, Oz started the first of many church building projects he directed on Taiwan. Christians gave gold, silver, and clothing to the building fund. One church member even offered to sell her blood to the hospital for transfusions so she could give more money.

In Taipei Mary stayed busy at home. As many as a hundred people crowded into her living room for English Bible classes. Besides taking care of Mary Lou and John, Mary also now had Tim and Linda. They were born in Taipei just a year apart.

The Quick family's first furlough came in the summer of 1953. First they made a slow voyage across the Pacific. Then they drove all the way from California to Missouri.

Long before daybreak each morning, Oz and Mary moved four sleepy little Quicks from a motel or hotel to makeshift beds in the back of a station wagon. The easiest part of the day's drive was before breakfast. As the hours stretched longer, everybody got hotter and louder and more weary.

Finally one day the station wagon rolled along a familiar river valley. "Mary Lou," said Oz, "when we cross that bridge up yonder and go on down the road a little ways, we'll be in Hardin, Missouri."

Mary Lou was not quite five years old. She looked up at Oz, her eyes bright with wonder. "Daddy," she breathed, "how in the world did you ever find it?"

By the end of that furlough, Mary had gathered all the books she needed to teach Mary Lou at home, like other missionary kids are taught by their mothers all over the world. But on their way back to Taiwan, the Quicks were asked to move down the island to Taichung [tie-JOONG]. When they got there, Morrison Academy was ready to open. It was planned especially for MKs. Mary Lou went to school at Morrison from the first grade through the twelfth. So did all the other Quick children.

The Quick kids' favorite missionaries were "Aunt Mary" and "Aunt Tillie." Mary Sampson and Lorene Tilford moved to Taichung to work with students.

Oz had just finished having a new house built for his family. One day he said, "Mary, this house would be a better place for the single missionaries to live."

Mary nodded. "It's closer to the university, isn't it?"

At first Aunt Mary and Aunt Tillie didn't want to take over the Quicks' brand-new house. But, finally, they did. Ever after, each time the Quicks came to visit, the two women would say, "Welcome home!"

One year Oz invited the two missionaries for breakfast on his birthday. But he didn't tell his wife about it. Mary wondered why her guests looked puzzled when she offered them only a cup of coffee. Gradually she realized they were expecting to eat at the Quicks', so she scurried toward the kitchen. It seemed the cook knew something she didn't: Mary saw ice cream and cake all ready. Finally Oz brought out a basket of packages wrapped in newspapers. He had a gift for every person there!

Another year Oz invited the two women to come over on

Lorene Tilford's birthday. Strange, he asked them to come at two o'clock, in the heat of the day. They soon found out why: Oz had gotten tickets to the circus for all six Quicks, and for Aunt Mary and Aunt Tillie too!

One day Oz was riding his motorcycle in Taichung when somebody shouted, "Hey, Chaplain Quick!"

The man had been the colonel of Oz's regiment in World War II. "Why don't you start English-language services for families of our soldiers stationed here?" he asked. Oz did, in addition to preaching in Chinese at a dozen other places.

Another furlough, and the four little Quicks had become five, born in four different countries. Sally joined the family at Kansas City in September of 1960.

That was the year the Quicks had two Christmases. Their ship was scheduled to leave before December 25, so they celebrated Christmas early with grandparents and aunts and uncles and cousins in Missouri. Then there turned out to be many friendly older passengers on the ship. They showered the young Quicks with three or four Christmas presents each.

Back in Taiwan again, Oz and Mary shook their heads to see the world's biggest outdoor Buddha being built not far from their home. "It's to protect us from floods like those we had last year," Buddha worshipers explained.

But many people of Taiwan were turning away from their idols. In a village on the west coast stood the main temple of Ma Tsu, goddess of the sea. Once a week Oz and a Taiwanese pastor traveled thirty miles to tell the good news in that pagan village. And the Baptist chapel there grew and grew.

One worshiper of Ma Tsu bought an old church building when the congregation moved out. Later he rented it to the

Baptists. One by one his children began attending services. Then his wife came, and finally the man himself. After becoming a Christian, he said to Oz, "I had to buy a church to hear the gospel!"

Once Oz saw a woman holding sticks of burning incense before a sidewalk table in front of an appliance store. On the table lay rice, a cooked chicken, and other sacrifices. Inside the store, two Taiwanese Christians joined Oz in telling the woman about Jesus. As soon as she became a believer, she asked them, "Can you talk to a friend of mine?"

Another time Oz and Mary brought home in the trunk of their car a clay image and paper pictures of Buddha and two other gods. A family had asked the Quicks to help them get rid of their idols.

Morrison Academy moved to a new campus that had a little idol shrine on one corner of it. Finally the school got permission to tear it down. But who would do it? Some Chinese wondered if some evil god or spirit would get angry? Oz Quick, a member of the school board, soon solved the problem. He climbed up on the roof of the tiny temple and started swinging a sledgehammer!

That wasn't the only time five young Quicks saw their dad in action as a missionary. Some of their favorite times were when they sailed to Green Island.

First came the long drive on steep, scary roads over the mountain backbone of Taiwan. Then they parked their car with friends on the east coast.

Early in the morning they boarded a fishing boat with a diesel motor. The voyage usually took only a few hours. But sometimes strong winds and high waves slowed them down. Once the islanders had to light firecrackers to guide the boat into harbor after dark!

On Green Island the Quicks camped upstairs over a

56

church building. They had no electric lights, no running water.

Oz used a generator to run his projector so he could show Christian films to the villagers. He visited people in prison. He helped Taiwan Baptist home missionaries working on Green Island.

Meanwhile, John and Tim and Linda explored the tiny island from one end to the other. They stuck their swimsuits under sun hats as they hiked down to the rocky seaside. They changed clothes and took a swim. They fished with bamboo poles. They hunted for shells. At sunset they gathered to watch boats pull in to shore with catches of sharks and fish.

Another trip the Quick children enjoyed was to go with their dad to Grandma Wang's orphanage. Grandma Wang loved children. She started taking in kids nobody else wanted. Before long, she had a houseful, and she had to start looking for a place with more room.

Christians in Taiwan and in America began helping Grandma Wang with her work. One who helped was Oz Quick. He went to tell the orphans about Jesus, who loves all the children of the world.

Another orphanage Oz and his children visited was farther up in the mountains. To get there they had to cross a narrow swinging bridge over a valley 150 feet deep.

One of the unwanted children at the mountain orphanage was a little girl born with no arms. How the older children loved her! They looked after her as if she were a favorite younger sister. Linda Quick could hardly believe it when she saw the little girl use her toes to tear off a candy wrapper. It was amazing that she kept her sleeping mat and blanket as neat as anyone else's in the big orphanage dormitory.

After Linda started to college in America, she came back to Taiwan one summer to visit her parents. She hadn't forgotten about the orphans either. With two members of the U.S. Army Medical Corps, Linda went out to help at the mountain orphanage. All day long she and her friends gave shots, cleaned cuts, and put salve on infected bites.

Through the years in Taiwan, Mary Quick worked with Baptist women in churches and chapels. She organized church youth groups; sometimes her own sons and daughters were among the members. Sometimes she played the organ for worship services. Sometimes she made visits for the church by foot, bicycle, motorcycle, or car.

After many happy years in Taichung, Oz and Mary moved still farther down the island, to the big seaport of Kaohsiung [gow-SHOONG]. Still later, they helped revive two churches at Hwalien [hwah-lee-EN], where city sidewalks are paved with marble chips from quarries in the mountains nearby.

One by one the five Quick children left home and started to college in the United States. One by one they came back to Taiwan for visits, in the summer or at Christmastime. Sometimes they brought boyfriends or girl friends with them. One by one they started getting married. By the summer of 1979, Oz and Mary Quick were grandparents.

Back to the Mainland,
Then to Missouri

"Mary," said Oz one day, "how would you like to go back to China?"

It was August 1981. Mainland China still wasn't letting in any missionaries, but tourists were different.

Mary and Oz Quick were ready to retire. But first they spent twelve happy days in China again. When they got to Kweilin, who should they meet but some of the church members they had known thirty-three years before!

"How's your baby, Mrs. Quick?" asked the Chinese Christians. "We've been praying for her all these years, but we never heard any news."

Mary got out photos of her beautiful daughter. Mary Lou now had two babies of her own. "You see, God does answer prayer," said Mary.

The pastor at Kweilin had died in a Communist prison, but his wife and children were still alive. Oz and Mary saw them in Shanghai.

Also in Shanghai, Oz met again two of the college students who had lived with him in Kweilin after Mary had gone home with Mary Lou. Like many others, they had suffered because of staying true to Christ.

The two old friends then mentioned still another of those

young men who had lived with Oz during the strike at the university.

"Poor Greg," they said.

Oz and Mary thought they were about to tell of someone else who had been persecuted or thrown in jail or even killed.

"Poor Greg," the Chinese Christians said. "He lost his faith."

Oz and Mary looked at each other. They knew that for their friends in China following Jesus meant more than anything else on earth. And they knew they could go home to Missouri now because other people would keep on telling the good news about Jesus in China, in Japan, in the Philippines, and especially, in Taiwan.

MANCHURIA
JAPAN
TOKYO
PEKING
CHINA
SHANGHAI
TAIPEI
TAICHUNG
HWALIEN
TAIWAN
KWEILIN
GREEN ISLAND
CANTON
KAOHSIUNG
HONG KONG
BAGUIO
PHILIPPINES
DAGUPAN
MANILA
VIETNAM
SAIGON

Remember

Oz Quick once said:

"God has taught me much: what it's like to be hungry; how to be frightened and not give in to fear; that there are questions which neither I nor any other human can answer.

"I learned the lesson of change. God's Word does not change, but social and political situations do, and mission work is done in the midst of change.

"Never has the Lord forsaken me . . . although he has let me sweat out some hard times."

Can you remember when Oz Quick learned each of these "lessons"? What can you learn from things that happen to you?

Mary Quick once said:

"I've had an exciting life. I praise the Lord for all he's done. Seek the Lord's will because this is where the excitement is. It's important to be at the right place at the right time. It's done through prayer.

"It's exciting to think about what could be done. The Lord is still saying, 'Whom shall I send? Who will go for us?' Our time has gone by quickly, and so will yours. Make the most of it now!"

Can you remember some of the exciting events in Mary Quick's life? Can you think of ways to take the good advice she has given you?

About the Author

When I was a sixth grader, my mother and I traveled by train to a big Baptist meeting in Danville, Kentucky. There I heard a young missionary who had an exciting story to tell. His name was easy to remember: Oz Quick.

Forty years later I met Mary Quick. We sat in their home in Liberty, Missouri, and ate a Chinese meal together. We looked through stacks of old photographs, diaries, letters, and their story became even more exciting. I could hardly wait to put it in a book.

Since 1965, Betty and I have been missionaries in Indonesia, to the south of Taiwan where the Quicks used to live. We have two grownup sons, Tim and Jamie. My main job is at the Indonesian Baptist Publishing House in Bandung [BAHN-doong]. But like most missionaries, Betty and I have done many different kinds of work.

This is the forty-eighth book I have written. Probably you can't read any of the twenty-seven books in Indonesian. Here are some of the twenty others in English: *A Bible Dictionary for Young Readers, Bible Guidebook, Church in the Big Top, Sing His Song Around the Earth, Judges and Kings: God's Chosen Leaders, To Be the First: Adventures of Adoniram Judson,* and *Indian Treasure on Rock House Creek.*